Being Mindful

Contents **Page**

I0869048

written by Samantha Montgomerie

Red Rocket Readers™

Engineered by Flying Start Books

Our minds are very busy. We think about what we see, what others have said, and about things that go on.

The cactus is a plant that has water inside. Other plants grow long roots to get water from deep underground.

Some small animals live in the desert. In the daytime, they hide under rocks or the sand to keep out of the sun.

At nighttime when it gets cold, they come out to find food and water.

Birds that live in the desert like to get away from the heat, too. Some fly high in the sky all day. Some birds only come out at night to find water and food.

Ostriches live in the deserts in Africa.
They are the biggest birds in the world.

Camels are large animals that can walk for many days without food or water.

People ride camels across the desert, or they use them to carry things.

Not many people live in deserts. It is hard to find water. Some people live in huts or tents.

They have sheep and goats to get wool, meat, and milk.

An oasis is a green place in the middle of a desert. Trees, grass, and plants grow there because it has some water. People can grow food. They make their homes with bricks made of mud.

oasis

Deserts can be windy. The sand blows around in sandstorms. People need clothes that are long and loose because of the sun, wind, and sand. They need warm clothes at night.